SERAFIMA'S ICONS

A NOVELLA

by **Leslie Donovan**
illustrated by **Fr. Jerome Sanderson**

LIGHT & LIFE PUBLISHING MINNEAPOLIS, MN

Light & Life Publishing Company
P.O. Box 26421
Minneapolis, Minnesota 55426-0421

Copyright © 2008
Light & Life Publishing Company

ISBN: 978-1-933654-21-8
Library of Congress Control Number: 2008932608

Humbly dedicated to the children of Russia:

DA KHRANIT VAS BOG!
GOD KEEP YOU!

*Royalties from this book will be donated to the
Decani Monastery Relief Fund in Kosovo*

ONE

The clothing market adjoining Izmailovsky Park bustled with activity. Vendors touted everything from blue jeans to business suits, while cooks at Uzbek eateries hawked their spicy delights. Occasionally, a hand would emerge from this or that darkened stall to grip the arm of an unwary customer, who would then be showered with attention by a merchant eager to boost sales. *Kvas* stands offered nourishing refreshment to thirsty passersby parched by the clouds of dust and the summer heat.

Even if she were rich, Serafima reflected as she examined a long rust-colored skirt, she would still prefer the market to Moscow's more upscale shops. The noisy chaos that surrounded her was far more exciting for an eleven-year-old girl than was the stuffy order of an expensive boutique.

"What do you think of this one, Aunt Masha?" asked Serafima, holding up the skirt for inspection. Aunt Masha had been very kind to Serafima since that terrible day when a car accident took the girl's mother from this world. Even though she was sometimes cross or distant with others, Aunt Masha was always warm and affectionate with Serafima.

"Oh, very nice! It goes well with your red hair, and your blue eyes, and," Aunt Masha added mischievously, "your freckles!" Serafima cringed. She hated having freckles, and she hated even more for anyone to notice them.

Serafima considered the three hundred rouble price tag on the skirt. She always liked to bring a little change home to her father, knowing how hard he worked, and he had given her only three hundred roubles to take to the market. "Perhaps I can mend my old black one," she said aloud to no one in particular.

"For you, two hundred fifty," said the merchant, a dark-haired lady whose tiredness showed through her apparent enthusiasm for making the sale. The price was right, and Serafima paid for the skirt, very pleased that she could return a whole fifty roubles to her father.

Distracted by her moment of shopping success, Serafima failed to notice the heavily-laden porter who was hurtling toward her. Nor could she hear his shouts of "Make way! Make way!" above the din of the marketplace. Before Serafima knew what was happening, a carpet roll bundled onto the porter's cart caught the back of her legs and sent her sprawling on the ground.

"Idiot!" yelled Aunt Masha, shaking her fist at the porter as he continued speeding through the dense crowd.

"Oh, don't be so hard on him, Aunt Masha," Serafima said as she dusted herself off. "He's probably come here all the way from Tashkent or Dushanbe hoping to make a little money so that his children at home can survive."

Aunt Masha smiled at her niece. "You're such a sweet girl," she said. "Why don't you take some of that change and buy yourself something nice to eat?"

"Do you think Papa would mind?" asked Serafima.

"Not at all, angel. He'd give you the world if he could."

Serafima took twenty roubles and bought two huge, juicy apples, her favorite fruit, from a fruit stand near the long row of currency exchanges at the market's entrance. She gave one of the apples to Aunt Masha, but the other she put into her bag so that she would have a treat for the next day. Tomorrow her father was taking her for a walk in the beautiful Alexandrovsky Gardens, and she was very excited.

TWO

Father Nikolai nervously ran his fingers through his reddish beard as he lay in bed, his heart pounding and his sheets damp with sweat. He'd been having *that* dream again, the one that had been hounding him for so long. He'd been dreaming about The Mouth.

What made Father Nikolai's nocturnal torment so disturbing was that his nightmare was no mere figment of imagination. He had met The Mouth while passing by Danilovsky Monastery. Turning aside in response to a low groan, he had seen an elderly woman sitting in the grass, directly under the large icon of St. Serafim of Sarov that is written onto the monastery's outer wall.

Seeing the woman's wretched state, Father Nikolai had offered her a packet of bread from the monastery's shop. It was then that the beggar had opened wide her foul Mouth and pointed to her two yellowed teeth, as if to say that she could not possibly chew such hard bread. His blood suddenly running cold, Father Nikolai had quickly rooted in his pockets for some spare change, tossed a few roubles into the woman's hand, and departed hastily without so much as offering a word of comfort.

Now, a year later, Father Nikolai stared up at the cracked ceiling of his room and marvelled that he was still dreaming about the poor *babushka* whom the wiles of the night had transformed into a nameless, featureless Mouth. Like wisps of moisture condensing into a droplet on cold glass, all of his fears had become concentrated in the image of that rotten, gaping Mouth.

Father Nikolai felt lost without Olga. He had spent the three years since his wife's death in a fog of exhaustion. The pressures of making ends meet in one of the world's most expensive cities while ministering to a small, poor congregation on the outskirts of Moscow overwhelmed him. But more than anything, he worried about the future of his only child in a constantly changing Russia.

The priest smiled a rare smile at the thought of his daughter. She was the one true joy in his life and a powerful sign for him that there is a God who loves mankind. No matter how deeply Father Nikolai was grieving, gentle Serafima could always lift his spirits.

His strength renewed by the prospect of taking Serafima on a special outing, Father Nikolai rose and began to wash himself. He even laughed out loud when he saw himself in the bathroom mirror. In order to save money, he sometimes had Father Oleg, a friend from his seminary days, trim his hair for him. Father Oleg had a kind heart but clumsy hands and the reflection that greeted Father Nikolai that morning sported long, flowing hair cut every which way.

A quiet, peaceful morning in Alexandrovsky Gardens with Serafima was just what he needed, Father Nikolai thought. By the time he began his morning prayers, he had managed to forget all about The Mouth.

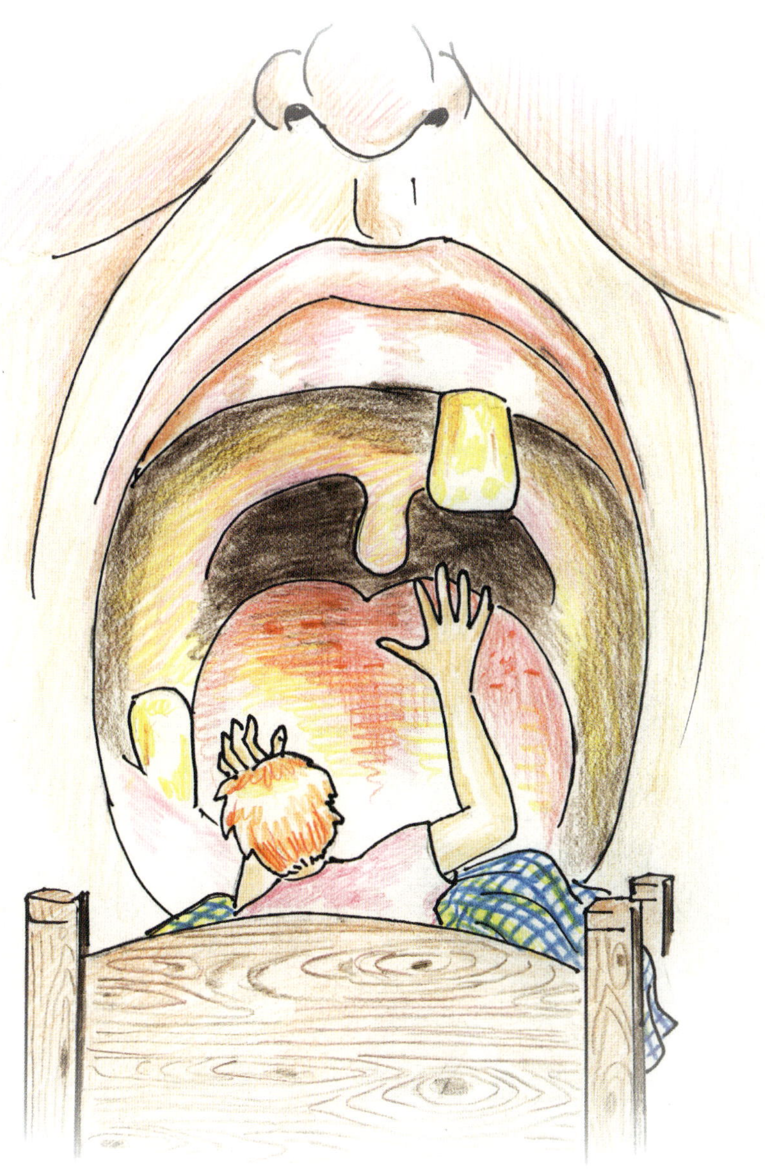

THREE

The sun was warm in Alexandrovsky Gardens, even though it was still early morning, and the earth was richly fragrant. Father Nikolai hoped that he and Serafima wouldn't need the black umbrella that stuck awkwardly out of one corner of his rucksack, but he knew that there was nothing more unpredictable than Moscow weather.

Serafima was especially delighted by the multitude of sparrows that chattered noisily and hopped along the ground near the bench where she sat next to her father. Once, she had seen such birds eat french fries right out of a tourist's hand at the nearby Okhotny Ryad Shopping Center. It comforted her to think of how God always gave such little creatures the things they needed to live. She, after all, was a little creature too.

But for Serafima, the best part of the outing was simply being with her father, sometimes talking with him about everything under the sun and at other times just resting quietly with him. Now, having finished his picnic lunch, Father Nikolai put his arm around his daughter's shoulders and she cuddled comfortably next to him. His warmth and his smell made her feel safe.

"Papa," she asked, "can we walk down to Saint Basil's?"

"We don't have enough money for tickets," Father Nikolai said. The much-celebrated Cathedral of the Protection of the Theotokos operated as a museum, with admission charged at the door. One day, Father Nikolai thought, he would like to take Serafima there to venerate the relics of Blessed Basil the holy fool, but that would have to wait.

"I know we can't go inside," said Serafima, "but I like just being near that church and looking at it."

Father Nikolai nodded in agreement and the two set off along the Kremlin wall, passing though the gates at the Corner Arsenal Tower and coming to the front of the State History Museum. Serafima was much amused by the unusually tall young man in front of the museum, who did not seem overly enthusiastic about his present role as Tsar Peter the Great.

Father and daughter were just about to enter Red Square through the Resurrection Gate when Serafima stopped short and gazed at the small chapel to their right. At first, Father Nikolai thought Serafima was drawn to the magnificent voices praising God within the chapel. But then he saw that her eyes were fixed on a young girl standing on the chapel steps.

The scrawny, unkempt girl was about Serafima's age and wore a faded sky-blue dress. In her hands, she held an icon of St. Serafim tending to the bear he once befriended at his Sarov hermitage. Her sad gray eyes stared blankly, as if they had seen too much grief for their tender age.

Serafima left her father standing beside the Resurrection Gate while she walked up to the girl, crossed herself, and kissed the icon of St. Serafim. Then, much to the girl's surprise, Serafima tried to strike up a conversation with her. "My name's Serafima," she said. "What's yours?"

"I'm . . . I'm Anna," the girl answered shyly. Anna smiled weakly at Serafima despite her shock at being greeted so warmly.

"Are there many children in your family, Anna?" Serafima asked.

"I'm the oldest of six," Anna replied.

Serafima suddenly remembered that she had forgotten to eat the apple so carefully packed in anticipation of today's picnic. She withdrew the apple from her bag and offered it to Anna.

"Oh! Thank you so much!" exclaimed Anna, her gray eyes sparkling in the morning sunlight.

Serafima took her leave of Anna and rejoined her father. Father Nikolai did not know what to make of his daughter's spontaneous act of generosity, but he said nothing about it as they passed through the Resurrection Gate together.

FOUR

Serafima had no sooner entered Red Square with her father than she went off to investigate another group of historical actors. Just then, Father Nikolai, who remained standing near the icon shop inside the Resurrection Gate, felt a gentle tug at the hem of his cassock. "For the sake of Christ, help me holy Father," a voice pleaded.

Father Nikolai squirmed uncomfortably. Somehow, he didn't feel very holy at all. He was horrified when he looked down and saw a young man about his own age seated on the ground, a wild-haired fellow with one leg cut off at the knee and the other leg entirely amputated.

"Can you spare some change, Father? One rouble? Two roubles?"

Father Nikolai glanced at Serafima, who was talking animatedly with a rather convincing Tsar Ivan the Terrible look-alike. Turning back to the beggar, who was so obviously in need, he felt pity for the man and began to search in his pockets for some coins.

Having managed to produce one rouble and fifty kopecks and to extend a gesture of blessing, Father Nikolai supposed that he ought to speak with the man as Serafima had with Anna. He was about to ask the man his name when a sickening thought caused his words to stick in his throat.

Instead of beginning a conversation, Father Nikolai nodded curtly and turned away to search for Serafima. He began to wish he had never agreed to take his daughter to Red Square. All he wanted was to leave the area as quickly as possible.

What had so unsettled the young priest was the thought that it could so easily have been himself huddled there on the ground, maimed and begging for alms. If he had not been in the seminary, if he had been recruited to fight in Chechnya . . . The more he tried to force such images from his mind, the more he found his thoughts racing back to the outer wall of Danilovsky Monastery and the black cavern of a Mouth that threatened to swallow him whole.

FIVE

While Father Nikolai had been searching for some change to offer the legless man, Serafima had left the actors at the side door of the State History Museum and made her way to Kazan Cathedral, which lies where Nikolskaya Street meets Red Square. Father Nikolai found her facing the cathedral entrance and he thought that perhaps she would like to go inside and pray.

Father Nikolai joined his daughter and took her hand. For some reason, Serafima made no motion to enter the church, but instead remained standing outside, her eyes fixed on the cathedral's concrete stairs. Or rather, Serafima's gaze was glued to the hunched figure occupying the top step, a woman.

And what a woman! She was eighty if she was a day, and she wore a gaudy dress patterned with orange and purple flowers. Her eyes were clouded over and her face lined and sunken. But perhaps her most outstanding feature was her hair, a greasy gray waterfall that cascaded over her bony shoulders and down to her waist.

"Look at her," Serafima said to her father. "She's so . . ." Father Nikolai shot Serafima a reproving glance, expecting her to say something rude. "She's so beautiful. She looks just like Saint Mary of Egypt, except with clothes on, of course."

Serafima regarded the motionless figure a moment longer. "She looks so sad, Papa. What will we do to help her?" she asked.

At any other time, Father Nikolai would have been angry at Serafima for asking such a question. After all, he couldn't very well feed all of Moscow, could he? But Father Nikolai suddenly found his heart filled with tender feeling. Tears, unbidden, began to form in the corners of his eyes. "I don't know, my little angel," he said. "You teach me."

SIX

Serafima confidently climbed the stairs leading to Kazan Cathedral. Although sitting on steps and sidewalks is frowned upon in Russia, she seated herself next to the withered woman. Taking his cues from his daughter, Father Nikolai sat down on the other side of the colorfully-dressed *babushka*.

"Good morning," ventured Serafima. The woman did not respond and her glassy eyes stared off into the distance, as if she could see through the Kremlin wall at the opposite side of the square to points far distant.

"My name is Serafima. What's yours?" Still, there was no reply. Serafima wondered if the old woman was deaf. In any case, she didn't seem much interested in conversation. Determined, Serafima decided she would have to try a different tack.

"When I feel sad, I always find that a hug helps." The woman remained unresponsive when Serafima first embraced her. But suddenly, the old lady picked Serafima up under the arms and swung the girl onto her lap as if Serafima weighed no more than a feather.

"I love children!" the *babushka* exclaimed in a surprisingly sweet voice. Serafima was amazed at woman's hidden reserve of strength. "My name is Anastasia Mikhailovna."

Father Nikolai, who had also been startled by Anastasia's sudden burst of affection, introduced himself and apologized for having nothing to offer her. Anastasia indicated the tin can in her gnarled hand and said, "Don't feel bad. I just collect a few roubles from foreigners every now and again to feed my cats. Those furry rascals are my only companions nowadays." She shrugged as if such loneliness had become routine to her.

"It's different for folks like Sergei," she continued. "He's desperate."

"Sergei?" asked Father Nikolai.

"The man with no legs who begs over in the corner," said Anastasia, motioning toward the icon shop with her head. "He needs every kopeck he can get his hands on, but I manage to survive on my pension."

"Now," said Anastasia to Father Nikolai, "your daughter gave me a nice warm hug. Do you suppose you could give me a blessing?"

Father Nikolai only just managed to offer a brief prayer asking God to grant Anastasia everything necessary for the good of her soul and body before he began to cry in earnest. Serafima, who had never seen her father cry, even when Mama died, was deeply troubled.

"Papa! Papa! What's the matter? Please don't cry," she pleaded.

"Shhh!" interjected Anastasia. "Leave your father in peace. He needs to cry so that he can be happy."

"But, Anastasia Mikhailovna, that makes no sense!" Serafima bit her tongue, hoping she didn't sound too rude. "I'm sorry. I mean, I just don't understand."

"Some tears," said Anastasia, "are a gift from God. Just as the rain washes the earth, tears of repentance cleanse the soul and make it holy."

"But Papa is very holy!" Serafima replied indignantly. "He's a priest!"

Anastasia smiled a knowing smile, but said nothing.

SEVEN

After a long silence, Anastasia began to speak again. "You're very blessed to have a priest for a father. I suppose you attend Divine Liturgy often?"

"As often as I can," answered Serafima. All this time, Father Nikolai sat with his face buried in his hands, his chest and shoulders heaving with muffled sobs.

Anastasia hung her head. "I want more than anything in the whole wide world to go to Divine Liturgy," she said.

Serafima was puzzled. Sometimes grownups were so hard to figure out! "You're sitting on the steps of a cathedral," said Serafima. "Why can't you go to Divine Liturgy?"

"Oh," Anastasia lamented, "my poor legs are not so strong for standing on anymore. Besides . . ." Anastasia hesitated. She looked away from Serafima. "Who wants an ugly old Baba Yaga like myself in church anyway?"

Father Nikolai removed his hands from his tearstained face. "Who would want to suffer for the sake of a miserable sinner like me?" he said. "Yet, Christ died for my sake." Casting a quick glance at the clock on the Kremlin's Saviour Tower, he rose shakily and went to check the schedule of services at Kazan Cathedral.

"In ten minutes . . ." Father Nikolai said, returning to his place on the step beside Anastasia, " . . .in ten minutes, all three of us will go to Divine Liturgy together, right here at Kazan Cathedral."

Anastasia's aged face beamed with joy. "You can lean on Serafima," Father Nikolai continued, "and you can also take my hand if you feel unsteady." Even as he said this, he suspected that Anastasia's legs would hold up just fine if only she was made to feel welcome in church.

EIGHT

"We who mystically represent the cherubim, and sing the Thrice-Holy Hymn to the life-giving Trinity, now lay aside all cares of life," intoned Father Nikolai along with the rest of the congregation. Indeed, he had not felt so light and carefree for many years.

Anastasia was more than holding her own. In fact, she crossed herself with a vigor that belied her advanced age. Serafima stood close by Anastasia and gave the responses in her sweet, birdlike voice.

Never had Father Nikolai's senses been so entirely transfigured. "Holy, holy, holy, Lord God of Sabaoth," resounded in his ears as if he were hearing choirs of angels. The pungent clouds of incense were a medicinal balm poured out on the wounds of his suffering soul.

And the icons: for Father Nikolai, these truly became windows into heaven. Each time he crossed himself, his eyes returned to the copy of St. Andrei Rublev's Holy Trinity icon that graces Kazan Cathedral. The rich glow of yellow ochre illuminated the serene faces of the three figures regarding each other in perfect unity and love.

At last, Father Nikolai understood that his daughter had shown him another sort of icon. Serafima's icons were written not in tempera, but in flesh and blood. In the poor of Moscow, she saw the face of Christ Himself.

NINE

It seems that not long after Father Nikolai's providential meeting with Anastasia, a multitude of legends began to circulate in his parish and beyond regarding his remarkable transformation. Some claimed to have seen him floating in the air and radiating a heavenly glow as he offered the Divine Liturgy "on behalf of all and for all." Others said that he was able to travel on foot in any sort of weather without becoming wet or cold. A few even insisted that they had seen him walking across the surface of the Moscow River, deep in intimate conversation with Saint Nicholas the Wonderworker.

The accuracy of such reports remains unknown, but this matters little, for it is certain that the change in Father Nikolai was nothing short of miraculous. These days he and Serafima can often be found wandering the streets of Moscow, tending to the poorest of the poor. They don't always have food in their bags or coins in their pockets, but they're never found without prayers, kind words, and listening ears.

There are two of their beloved icons of Christ, however, whom Serafima and Father Nikolai never visit without bringing something special to eat. The first of these is The Mouth. Having returned to Danilovsky Monastery to find that The Mouth has a name, Tatiana Grigorevna, and a story of her own, father and daughter bring her soft, nourishing *kashas* whenever they can.

The other is Anastasia. Sometimes Serafima and her father visit Anastasia's humble room, where Serafima likes to romp and play with Anastasia's cats, Boris and Ivan. Anastasia, Serafima, and Father Nikolai occasionally attend Divine Liturgy together at Kazan Cathedral, and Sergei and Anna have been known to join them.

It just might happen that if you frequent Moscow's busy streets, you will come upon Father Nikolai and Serafima ministering to the poor. Serafima, who grows daily not only in stature but also in wisdom, is unmistakable with her red hair, her bright blue eyes, and, of course, her freckles. Father Nikolai's long reddish hair is always trimmed to at least five different lengths, as he is still good friends with Father Oleg. And if you should encounter these two humble servants of God as they go about their work, consider yourself very blessed indeed.

One more thing must be said regarding Father Nikolai, something that up until now has been known only to those who love him best. Since he began to empty himself in the service of the poor, he hasn't had a single unpleasant dream. Instead, he falls into a peaceful, holy sleep each night, surrounded by the angels God Himself so graciously sends to guard each and every one of us in His divine love.

GLOSSARY

Baba Yaga: A cruel, ugly witch character in Russian folktales.

Babushka: Literally, "grandmother"; an elderly woman.

Cassock: A long black robe worn by priests.

Chechnya: A region of southern Russia that suffers from ongoing conflict.

Dushanbe: The capital city of Tajikistan, which is a country in Central Asia.

Hermitage: The place where a hermit lives in prayerful solitude.

Holy Fool: A person who lives in total poverty for the sake of Christ and uses strange behavior to show that God's love is what really matters.

Kasha: Any one of many varieties of hot cereal.

Kopeck: A unit of Russian money. There are one hundred kopecks in a rouble.

Kvas: A bitter drink made from rye bread.

Providential: Coming from God's unconditional care and love for us.

Rouble: The basic unit of Russian money.

Tashkent: The capital city of Uzbekistan, which is a country in Central Asia.

Tempera: Paint used in iconography made from powdered pigments mixed with egg.

Uzbek: Describes a Central Asian people and their language. Many, but not all, Uzbeks live in Uzbekistan.

Yellow Ochre: An earthy-yellow pigment used extensively in iconography

GUIDE TO MOSCOW LOCATIONS

Alexandrovsky Gardens: This favorite relaxation spot is made up of a pleasant arrangement of flower beds, garden paths, and benches stretching along the west wall of the Kremlin. The gardens were designed in 1819-1823 by Osip Bove and planted on the former riverbed of the Neglinnaya River, which had been redirected underground. They take their name from Tsar Alexander I, who was in power when the garden was first created.

Danilovsky Monastery: Moscow's first monastery was founded in 1282 by the grand prince St. Danil. Since 1982, this monastery has been the official residence of the Patriarch of the Russian Orthodox Church. Moscow's poor often gather along the outer wall of the monastery hoping that pilgrims will offer them alms.

Izmailovsky Park: This forest park was originally built in the early 1600s for Tsar Alexei Mikhailovich, and his grandson, Tsar Peter the Great, spent much of his childhood sailing there. Tourists and locals alike flock to the markets near the park, one featuring art and souvenirs and the other selling mainly clothing.

Kazan Cathedral: This Orthodox church in the northeast corner of Red Square was built in the early 1630s to celebrate a Russian victory over Poland. Destroyed under Stalin's rule in 1936, this cathedral was the first such church in Russia to be completely rebuilt. The present Kazan Cathedral was copied from drawings of the original and constructed in 1990-1993.

The Kremlin: The Kremlin is a walled fortress on the Moscow River that has traditionally served as the center of Russian government, except for during the Imperial period when the capital was moved to St. Petersburg. The Kremlin contains four palaces and four cathedrals, and it is the residence of the current president of Russia. The earliest fortress on this site was built in the twelfth century and the present walls and towers were constructed in 1485-1495.

Red Square: The large square east of the Kremlin was originally a market, and for centuries it has been at the heart of Russian history. St. Basil's Cathedral graces one end of the square, while the State History Museum lies at the other. Red Square was named not for the color of the bricks in the Kremlin wall, but for the fact that the Russian word for "red" used to mean "beautiful" in old Russian.

Resurrection Gate: This entrance to Red Square stands between Moscow City Hall and the State History Museum. It is sometimes called the Iberian Gate, and the small chapel near the gate is called the Iberian (Iverskaya) Chapel after its copy of an icon of the Theotokos whose original rests in the Georgian Iveron Monastery on Mount Athos. Resurrection Gate has traditionally been a place where everyone from royalty to beggars prayed together as they stopped to venerate the Iverskaya icon of the Mother of God before a visit to Red Square or the Kremlin.

Saint Basil's Cathedral: This colorful onion-domed church was founded in 1555-1561 by Tsar Ivan IV to celebrate Russia's victory over the Tatars in Kazan. Officially called the Cathedral of the Protection of the Theotokos, it is better known for the relics of the holy fool, Basil the Blessed, which repose there.

State History Museum: Founded in 1872, the State History Museum lies opposite St. Basil's Cathedral on Red Square and depicts the history of the Russian land from prehistoric to modern times.

SAINTS IN THE STORY

Below are a few brief notes on the holy men and women mentioned in *Serafima's Icons*. These are not meant to be full biographies; they are simply a starting point for learning more about these remarkable servants of God.

St. Andrei Rublev (died c. 1430)

Little is known for certain about this saint's life, but he is recognized as the iconographer who wrote the Holy Trinity icon for the Trinity-St. Sergius Monastery founded by St. Sergius of Radonezh. Andrei's gentleness and purity of heart come across in the gracefulness of his sacred art. The Holy Trinity icon depicts the Trinity in the form of the three angels who visited Abraham. The three figures look at each other with tender attention and perfect love. This icon expresses far more deeply than any words the spirituality of loving unity in the Trinity upon which St. Sergius founded his monastery. The original of this icon is now in the Tretyakov Gallery in Moscow.

Blessed Basil (died 1552)

Basil, treasured by his long-childless parents, showed great dedication to serving God at an early age and was granted the gift of forevision when he was very young. At the age of sixteen, he began to live as a fool for Christ's sake in Moscow, where he endured long winters dressed only in a long shirt. Basil comforted the poor and oppressed, but he sternly corrected those who did evil, including Tsar Ivan IV himself, with a courage that could only come from total trust in God's providence. Basil's relics filled Moscow with a wonderful fragrance when the saint fell asleep in Christ, and they now rest in the Cathedral of the Protection of the Theotokos, which is usually called St. Basil's Cathedral.

Fully-developed holy foolishness is a rare vocation, but all of us can learn from holy fools to examine our consciences and see if God truly holds first place in our lives. Children can learn from Blessed Basil the importance of prayer, fasting, and almsgiving in forming a tender heart open to the Spirit from one's earliest years.

St. Mary of Egypt (4th or 5th Century)

Mary was born in Alexandria, and in her youth she ignored God and committed many sins. Then, on a trip to Jerusalem, she found that she could not enter the Church of the Holy Sepulcher. She prayed before an icon of the Theotokos, and through the intercession of the Virgin Mary was able to fall before Christ's cross in tearful repentence. Later, she lived as a desert hermit, eventually clothed in nothing but her own long hair. She struggled in constant prayer for decades.

St. Mary's life calls all of us to turn away from our sins and seek God's forgiveness. Like the father in the Gospel who welcomed the prodigal son, God is ever eager to rejoice over sinners who seek His mercy.

St. Nicholas the Wonderworker (died 343)

The beloved bishop of Myra, friend of the poor, hope of prisoners, and protector of children, needs little introduction. As the patron saint of Russia, Nicholas is lovingly venerated throughout Russia and his icon may be seen everywhere in that country. His love of neighbor and his patience when imprisoned for his faith remain a model for Christians today. Nicholas is still a wonderworker for all who seek his loving intercession.

St. Serafim of Sarov (1759-1833)

Serafim's kindness, gentleness, and inner peace shine forth from the many icons of this Russian saint. After a youth filled with much prayer, he entered monastic life and eventually became a hermit. In the Sarov forest, Serafim devoted himself to the Jesus Prayer ("Lord Jesus Christ, Son of God, have mercy on me, a sinner.") and made friends with the animals, including a bear who took food from the saint's hands. He continued to grow in his relationship with God and came to be known far and wide as a *starets*, a holy elder able to understand the depths of people's hearts and help them on their spiritual journeys.

Serafim taught that the goal of Christian life is union with God: to acquire the Holy Spirit. Not only that, but he assures us that if we acquire the Spirit of peace, then a thousand souls around us will be saved. If all fell through the sin of our first parents, how much more can all be redeemed together through Christ's love and our cooperation with His plans for us!